The Authors

Maralene and Miles Wesner are multi-talented teachers and prolific writers. They have published more than 150 Audio-Visual Education aids, and pioneered new reading methods with their Phonics in a Nutshell (1965).

They have written articles, and mission studies for Southern Baptist periodicals. They were in the original group of writers to develop WMU's Big "A" Club material.

They've published several books with Broadman Press: *A Fresh Look at the Gospel* (1983); *You Are What You Choose* (1984); and *How To Be a Saint When You Feel Like a Sinner* (1986) and self-published 30 books by Diversity Press.

They are noted for their no-nonsense style, their clear illustrations, and their willingness to face controversial issues. From the dual perspectives of both academic and religious professions, they seek to be a bridge between the spiritual and the intellectual worlds.

They hold Masters Degrees (MEd) from Oklahoma University plus work toward a Doctorate. Miles also attended Southwestern Baptist Theological Seminary, and served as a high school counselor. He has been the bi-vocational pastor of a small rural church for more than 50 years.

Both Maralene and Miles taught in public school and collages and served as educational consultants. Maralene taught Psychology and Speech for Southeastern Oklahoma State University for 32 years. She was chosen Oklahoma Teacher of the Year in 1975.

They have planned, led tours, and done research in all of the 50 states, Canada, Mexico, Europe, Egypt, Japan, and the Holy Land. In 1985, they were among a small group of Americans who were invited by Dr. Joseph P. Kennedy of the US/China Education Foundation and Bishop Ting, leader of the Three Self Movement, to participate in the First Symposium on the Church in Nanjing, China.

Now, they use their lifetime of varied experiences to write insightful sermons, essays, and books.

Titles by Maralene & Miles Wesner
published by Nurturing Faith

Sermons for Special Days

Life More Abundant

Do You Really Know Jesus?

DO YOU *Really* KNOW JESUS?

Maralene & Miles Wesner

© 2021
Published in the United States by Nurturing Faith, Macon, GA.
Nurturing Faith is a book imprint of Good Faith Media (goodfaithmedia.org).
Library of Congress Cataloging-in-Publication Data is available.

ISBN: 978-1-63528-168-2

All rights reserved. Printed in the United States of America.

Scripture quotations are from New Revised Standard Version Bible, copyright © 1989 National Council of the Churches of Christ in the United States of America. Used by permission. All rights reserved worldwide.

Scriptures marked KJV are taken from the KING JAMES VERSION (KJV): KING JAMES VERSION, public domain.

Cover photograph by Bruce Gourley.

Contents

Preface 1

Chapter 1: Jesus Experienced Normal Growth 5

Chapter 2: Jesus Expressed Real Feelings 11

Chapter 3: Jesus Analyzed Deep Thoughts 17

Chapter 4: Jesus Spoke Wise Words 23

Chapter 5: Jesus Performed Good Deeds 27

Chapter 6: Jesus Possessed Common Sense 33

Chapter 7: Jesus Revealed the Nature of God 39

Chapter 8: Jesus Explained the Problem of Evil 45

Chapter 9: Jesus Promised the Possibility of Redemption ... 53

Chapter 10: Jesus Stressed the Importance of Concern 59

Chapter 11: Jesus Encouraged the Acceptance of Responsibility 65

Chapter 12: Jesus Defined the Duties of the Church 71

Conclusion: A Profile of Jesus 77

Preface

The question "Do you know Jesus?" elicits a common response among Christians: "Sure, I know Jesus!" But do we *really* know Jesus?

Knowing a few details about him is not enough. Marveling at his miraculous deeds is not enough. Most of us fail to realize that we're commanded to follow Jesus, to be like Jesus, and to carry out his message and ministry. In order to do this, we desperately need to know as many details as possible about his humanity.

We can't duplicate Jesus's divine powers, but we can—and must—duplicate his human qualities. To do this, we must know how he felt, how he thought, what he said, and what he did. We must examine his purposes, his attitudes, and his character traits. That's what we'll be discovering and emphasizing in this book.

We've spent months digging through red-letter editions of the Gospels, seeking out every clue and analyzing every incident that gives us information about Jesus as a person. It was a fascinating, eye-opening experience.

We found that many ideas people have about Jesus are just stereotypes and not based on the scriptures. He wasn't merely a religious icon. He certainly wasn't a pious fanatic. Instead, he was an interesting and vital individual. He expressed strong feelings of impatience, anger, and depression, as well as joy, sympathy, and love. He was a logical thinker. His teachings and stories emphasized concern for others and hatred for hypocrisy and greed. He was a man with a lot of common sense and humor.

In order to really know Jesus, we must develop an understanding of his human personality. We must come to know him as a friend as well as a savior. Unfortunately, very little research of this nature is available, and very few churches deal with these issues, but that's our theme! It's different, and we promise readers will make surprising discoveries and acquire new outlooks.

Understanding the meaning of his activities and achievements will help us know him better and become more like him. That's important because, according to the scripture, "Whoever says, 'I abide in him,' ought to walk just as he walked" (1 John 2:6).

Built by Herod around 20-10 BCE, Caesarea (also referred to as Caesarea Maritima), named after Caesar Augustus, was a town on the Mediterranean coast in north central Israel in the Providence of Judea, with Nazareth to the north and Samaria to the south. The town played a prominent role in the life of the early Christian Church. Pictured are ruins of the ancient town, today known as Caesarea National Park.
—*Photo copyright Bruce Gourley*

Chapter 1

Jesus Experienced Normal Growth

Most of us have heard that Jesus was born in Bethlehem and died on a cross near Jerusalem. We may even be able to quote some verses from his teachings, but few Christians have actually spent time studying the basic personality traits and belief system of this amazing man. In order to know people, we must understand their feelings, their thoughts, their words, their deeds, and their life purposes. Unfortunately, the Bible doesn't give us a neat list of Jesus's traits and characteristics. But the Gospels do give us some brief glimpses into his disposition and some small clues about his interests.

One momentous event occurred when Jesus was twelve years old. This journey to Jerusalem during a religious celebration would have been an exciting experience for any child. It certainly was for this boy from the little town of Nazareth.

The first thing we learn about Jesus is that he had a spirit of adventure and independence. He gets separated from his family and lost in the huge throngs of people. Surprisingly, he seems to be on his own for three days. Mary and Joseph were frantic as they searched among their relatives and friends. Strangely enough, he wasn't playing with his cousins or wandering through the many markets. Instead, the scriptures say, "They found him in the temple, sitting among the teachers, listening to them and asking them questions. And all who heard him were amazed at his understanding and his answers" (Luke 2:46–47).

The people didn't know what to make of this child prodigy. Even Mary and Joseph were bewildered His mother scolded him for giving them such a scare: "Child, why have you treated us like this? Look, your father and I have been searching for you in great anxiety" (Luke 2:48). Jesus replied, "Why were you searching for me? Did you not know that I must be in my Father's house?" (Luke 2:49). Jesus was an intelligent and verbal young man, already deeply interested in spiritual matters.

Jesus was obedient, and he developed—intellectually, physically, spiritually, and socially—in a normal manner. In fact, during his entire life he was considered to be an ordinary man. When he spoke in his community synagogue, the people were astonished and said, "Where did this man get this wisdom and these deeds of power? Is not this the carpenter's son? Is not his mother called Mary? And are not his brothers James and Joseph and Simon and Judas? And are not all his sisters with us? Where then did this man get all this?" (Matt 13:54–56).

Jesus presented himself as a normal person, not an eccentric religious zealot like John the Baptist, saying, "John came neither eating nor drinking, and they say, 'He has a demon'; the Son of Man came eating and drinking and they say, 'Look, a glutton and a drunkard, a friend of tax collectors and sinners!'" (Matt 11:18–19).

It's surprising that even at the end of his life, his appearance was so ordinary that Judas was paid by the soldiers to point him out in the crowd by saying, "The one I will kiss is the man; arrest him" (Matt 26:48).

Jesus's baptism was a high point of his life. It was an unusual event because baptism was not required of religious Jews. They claimed a special relationship to God because of their race and background. It was only outsiders wishing to adopt the Hebrew faith who were required to be baptized. Jesus's decision to submit to this ritual helped him identify with common and even alienated individuals who were seeking a more authentic relationship with God. That's why, when Jesus came for baptism, John refused, saying, "I need to be baptized by you, and do you come to me?" (Matt 3:14). But Jesus insisted: "Let it be so now; for it is proper for us in this way to fulfill all righteousness" (Matt 3:15).

In our lives, high points are usually followed by low points. After his baptism Jesus entered into an intense period of temptation. He was tempted by the need for food, the need for physical protection, and the desire for power and fame.

All of us have these basic needs and desires. The fact that Jesus was tempted shows evidence of his humanity. He overcame these temptations by relying on the scriptures. When Jesus was hungry,

> the tempter came and said to him, "If you are the Son of God, command these stones to become loaves of bread." But he answered, "It is written, 'One does not live by bread alone, but by every word that comes from the mouth of God.'" Then the devil took him to the holy city and placed him on the pinnacle of the temple, saying to him, "If you are the Son of God, throw yourself down; for it is written, 'He will command his angels concerning you,' and 'On their hands they will bear you up, so that you will not dash your foot against a stone.'" Jesus said to him, "Again it is written, 'Do not put the Lord your God to the test.'" Again, the devil took him to a very high mountain and showed him all the kingdoms of the world and their splendor; and he said to him, "All these I will give you, if you will fall down and worship me." Jesus said to him, "Away with you, Satan! for it is written, 'Worship the Lord your God, and serve only him.'" (Matt 4:3-10)

Luke says, "When the devil finished every test, he departed from him until an opportune time" (Luke 4:13). This indicates that Jesus continued to face temptations throughout his life. Jesus said he expected to be arrested and killed. Peter rebuked him, saying, "'God forbid it, Lord! This must never happen to you.' But he turned and said to Peter, 'Get behind me, Satan! You are a stumbling block to me'" (Matt 16:22–23).

After his forty days in the wilderness, Jesus spoke in his hometown synagogue. He explained his call to service by reading these words from Isaiah: "The Spirit of the Lord is upon me, because he has anointed me to bring good news to the poor. He has sent me to proclaim release to the captives and recovery of sight for the blind, to let the oppressed go free" (Luke 4:18).

Since his audience was made up of his friends and neighbors, at first they seemed pleased. But their responses quickly deteriorated into anger and violence. The moment he deviated from traditional beliefs, the people became furious. What on earth had he said to provoke such a reaction? He had simply repeated an Old Testament story, adding, "There were many widows in Israel…when the heaven was shut up three years and six months, and there was a severe famine over the land; yet Elijah was sent to none of them except to a widow…in Sidon. There were also many lepers in Israel at the time of the prophet Elisha, and none of them was cleansed except Naaman the Syrian" (Luke 4:25–27).

We may not understand why Jesus's statements were so controversial that they instigated a riot. But the widow of Sidon and the leper Naaman were not orthodox Jews. They were different. They were foreigners. Most Israelites believed God only favored them. They certainly didn't believe he accepted or blessed people of other religions and nationalities.

When Jesus spoke of God's acceptance *and* blessings toward these individuals, many "good," law-abiding people were disturbed. From that moment on, Jesus's overriding mission was established. His world-changing message included the surprising idea that God loves everybody, even those considered "different." In fact, he emphasized that God especially cares for those who are poor, brokenhearted, disabled, despised and condemned.

The stage was set for his strange and controversial teachings about accepting sinners, forgiving prostitutes, eating with tax collectors, praising Roman centurions, interacting with women, and calling Samaritans "good neighbors." Over and over, he stressed the fact that no one is excluded because of race, nationality, or culture. All people are called and loved by God. All people are to serve together.

Jesus explained his future plans, saying, "I have other sheep that do not belong to this fold. I must bring them also, and they will listen to my voice. So there will be one flock, one shepherd" (John 10:16). Such acceptance and broad-mindedness were unheard of twenty centuries ago; indeed, they are still unpracticed by most people today. It's unfortunate that these inclusive views are not considered to be basic doctrines in most churches, because they define Jesus's life and, to a great degree, explain his death.

Do you really know Jesus? Can you see him as a bright, eager twelve-year-old, anxious to listen and ask questions? Can you appreciate his willingness to be baptized with groups of common people? Can you identify with him when he is hungry and tempted to produce instant food? Or to perform miraculous feats as a way to attract and impress unbelievers? Can you sympathize with the deep hurts he felt when his own friends and neighbors tried to kill him? In short, can you truly grieve with him when he realizes his mission is going to be extremely difficult to carry out and his message is going to be totally rejected by millions of people?

If we can understand and empathize with Jesus, we will know him better and become more like him.

Chapter 2

Jesus Expressed Real Feelings

We don't really know individuals until we know how they feel about certain ideas and experiences. Yet few Christians notice or think about Jesus's feelings. He felt all the emotions we feel. It's reassuring to realize that our feelings are normal and legitimate. It's also helpful to find out what caused Jesus to have these feelings and to discover how he handled them. Everybody gets impatient, irritated, and aggravated. Everybody gets angry at times. Our stereotype of a meek and mild Jesus often prevents us from seeing the real Jesus.

When the disciples' lack of understanding was hindering Jesus's mission, Jesus complained, "You faithless and perverse generation, how much longer must I be with you? How much longer must I put up with you?" (Matt 17:17).

Jesus's frustration also became evident when a group of Jews questioned his authority. He responded sharply: "Why do you not understand what I say? It is because you cannot accept my word. You are from your father the devil, and you choose to do your father's desires" (John 8:43–44). Then, when Philip asked him to show them the Father, he replied, "Have I been with you all this time, Philip, and you still do not know me? Whoever has seen me has seen the Father. How can you say, 'Show us the Father'?" (John 14:9). On the night when he found his disciples sleeping in the garden of Gethsemane, Jesus complained, saying, "Could you not stay awake with me one hour?" (Matt 26:40).

Anger is a universal emotion. It can be useful or destructive. Jesus gave warnings about the improper use of anger, saying, "If you are angry with a brother or sister, you will be liable to judgment" (Matt 5:22). In the parable of the prodigal son, Jesus described a case of unjustified anger: "[The older son] became angry and…answered his father, 'Listen! For all these years I have been working like a slave for you…yet you have never given me even a young goat so that I might celebrate with my friends. But when this son of yours came back, who has devoured your property with prostitutes, you killed the fatted calf for him!'" (see Luke 15:28–30). This anger was wrong because it included personal jealousy and resentment.

However, in another parable Jesus tells of a man who seemed to have justifiable anger and used it in a productive way. When the people he had invited to a feast made excuses for rejecting his gracious invitation, the master became angry and said, "Go out at once into the streets and lanes of the town and bring in the poor, the crippled, the blind, and the lame…. Go out into the roads and lanes, and compel people to come in" (Luke 14:21–23).

On several occasions we actually see an angry Jesus. Once, when religious fanatics condemned him for healing on the sabbath, "he looked around at them with anger; he was grieved at their hardness of heart" (Mark 3:5). In fact, Jesus often became furious at self-righteous and deceitful leaders. When the Pharisees criticized him for breaking their rules, he said, "How can you speak good things, when you are evil?" (Matt 12:34). On another occasion he said, "Woe to you…hypocrites! For you cross sea and land to make a single convert, and you make the new convert twice as much a child of hell as yourselves…. You snakes, you brood of vipers! How can you escape being sentenced to hell?" (Matt 23:15, 33). Jesus's tirade to these smug scribes and Pharisees was harsh and severe. His anger once led to physical violence when money changers cheated the poor worshipers as they tried to buy sacrifices in the temple (see John 2:15–16).

It's important to note that Jesus never became upset over petty personal insults. Instead, his anger was always directed at moral issues. He became angry when priests were more concerned about their rules than they were about hurting people. He became angry at hypocrisy because it was dishonest and deceitful. He became angry at evil religious leaders who misled innocent people. He handled his anger by clearly expressing his displeasure and then doing what needed to be done to correct the situation. He didn't seek revenge. He didn't hold on to his resentment, and he didn't become bitter.

When we think of Jesus as God's son, the Messiah, and the savior of the world, it's hard to imagine that he could be discouraged and depressed. Yet he displayed these emotions on many occasions. Jesus was deeply disappointed at the people's lack of response, but he didn't let that affect his mission. He never gave up.

All of us experience tragedies and sorrow, but it's difficult to comprehend that a powerful person like Jesus would feel such grief, but he did. Jesus wept at the tomb of Lazarus (see John 11:35). Once he said, "My soul is troubled" (John 12:27). Later, the scriptures say, "[He] began to be grieved and agitated. Then he said to [Peter and the two sons of Zebedee], 'I am deeply grieved, even to death'" (Matt 26:37–38). In the garden of Gethsemane, Jesus was severely depressed. He didn't pretend. He didn't smile and say, "I'm fine." Instead, he fully expressed his feelings. He was in agony, and he admitted it.

Since we know that Jesus felt everything we feel, it's evident that elements of dread and fear were present in the garden and on the cross. Some of his last words show a depth of despair. Jesus cried out, "My God, my God, why have you forsaken me?" (Matt 27:46).

Because the Bible gives an honest account of Jesus's feelings, we know that experiencing grief and asking agonizing questions are not signs of a lack of faith. Fortunately, not all of Jesus's emotions were negative. We also see an excited, joyful Jesus (e.g., Luke 10:21). Some religions teach that pleasure is sinful, but Jesus said, "I have said these things to you so that my joy may be in you, and that your joy may be complete" (John 15:11; see also Luke 15:10, 32).

Other emotions that Jesus displayed were sympathy and compassion. Over and over, we read about Jesus's compassion. This suggests that his feelings motivated him to act in beneficial ways. Once, when Jesus saw a hungry crowd, he said, "I have compassion for the crowd, because they have been with me now for three days and have nothing to eat; and I do not want to send them away hungry, for they might faint on the way" (Matt 15:32). When a leper asked for healing, Jesus healed him (see Mark 1:41). When a woman lost her only son, Jesus healed her son (see Luke 7:13).

Finally, the one overwhelming emotion that defined Jesus's life and ministry is love. His love goes beyond pity and sympathy. It extends to forgiveness and grace. His love includes everybody, but he had a special affection for a few friends, such as Mary, Martha, and Lazarus. Also, despite the fact that the rich young ruler rejected Jesus's call and walked away, Jesus still loved him (see Mark 10:21). He must have recognized the great potential of this serious, honest seeker and was disappointed when he didn't respond. Jesus even felt a personal affinity for the soldiers who crucified him.

We've seen an impatient, irritated, and angry Jesus, but we learned that he didn't let these negative emotions consume his life or affect his ministry. His anger was never selfish or destructive. Instead, it was directed at the evil actions that hurt innocent people.

We've seen a discouraged, sorrowful, and depressed Jesus, but we learned that he didn't let his discouragement cause him to give up or lash out. He dealt with his dread of the crucifixion by choosing to accept God's will concerning the outcome.

Thankfully, we've also seen an excited and joyful Jesus, and his joy was shared with his associates as they celebrated together.

We've seen a sympathetic, compassionate, and loving Jesus. This compassion motivated him to heal, help, teach, and minister. His love enabled him to give his life for others.

Besides discovering something about Jesus's own personality, we have also learned how he handled these legitimate human emotions. Realizing that Jesus felt all the things we've felt gives us the freedom to admit and deal with our own feelings. We don't have to deny our anger. We don't have to hide our sorrow. We don't have to dampen our joy. We don't have to be embarrassed about our compassion and love. We now know that these feelings are normal and can be used in productive ways.

Researching and analyzing Jesus's emotions allows us to develop a relationship with him as a friend and a companion, as well as to acknowledge him as savior. Understanding how Jesus felt and seeing how he handled those feelings helps us know him better and become more like him.

Chapter 3

Jesus Analyzed Deep Thoughts

Jesus was an intelligent person, and he emphasized the importance of thoughts. He was also intuitive about other people's thoughts. Furthermore, Jesus was an astute thinker (see, e.g., Matt 21:24–27).

A person's thoughts reveal his character. Jesus's thoughts were always altruistic and unselfish. He even remembered to provide for his mother as he was dying on the cross (see John 19:25–27).

Jesus admired clever thinking. When a foreign woman asked for help, Jesus said, "I was sent only to the lost sheep of the house of Israel.... It is not fair to take the children's food and throw it to the dogs." Instead of pitifully begging, the woman boldly retorted, "Yes, Lord, yet even the dogs eat the crumbs that fall from their masters' table." Jesus was delighted by her wit, and rewarded her, saying, "Woman, great is your faith! Let it be done for you as you wish" (see Matt 15:24–28).

Jesus often posed questions that encouraged his disciples to think! After relating the parable of the good Samaritan, he asked, "Which of these three, do you think, was a neighbor to the man who fell into the hands of the robbers?" (Luke 10:36). When Peter was trying to decide what to do about paying taxes, Jesus said, "What do you think, Simon? From whom do kings of the earth take toll or tribute? From their children or from others?" (Matt 17:25). When emphasizing God's love for us, he asked, "What do you think? If a shepherd has a hundred sheep, and one of them has gone astray, does he not leave the ninety-nine on the mountains and go in search of the one that went astray?" (Matt 18:12).

On one occasion Jesus explained that it's actions, not empty words, that matter, saying, "What do you think? A man had two sons; he went to the first and said, 'Son, go and work in the vineyard today.' He answered, 'I will not'; but later he changed his mind and went. The father went to the second and said the same; and he answered, 'I go, sir'; but he did not go. Which of the two did the will of his father? They said, 'The first'" (see Matt 21:28–31).

Jesus also asked the important question many people ask when bad things happen to good people. Someone had informed Jesus about the Galileans whose blood Pilate had mixed with their sacrifices: "He asked them, 'Do you think that because these Galileans suffered in this way they were worse sinners than all other Galileans? No, I tell you; but unless you repent, you will all perish as they did. Or those eighteen who were killed when the tower of Siloam fell on them—do you think that they were worse offenders than all the others living in Jerusalem? No, I tell you'" (see Luke 13:2–5). Here, Jesus clearly refutes the widespread belief that all tragedies are punishments from God.

Jesus posed his most profound question to a group of Pharisees when he asked, "What do you think of the Messiah?" (Matt 22:42). That's a thought-provoking question, even today. Jesus insisted that our inner thoughts and our outer deeds must match. He understood that evil usually begins within the hearts and minds of individuals (see Mark 7:21–23). He agreed with Isaiah who said, "Let the wicked forsake their way, and the unrighteous their thoughts" (Isa 55:7). Jesus knew that thoughts are powerful and usually lead to actions. He realized that invisible things like hatred and lust are real. He knew that if we think evil, we'll inevitably bring it into our lives.

Jesus told a parable about a selfish and greedy man who used thought in an evil way, saying, "The land of a rich man produced abundantly. And he thought to himself, 'What should I do, for I have no place to store my crops?' Then he said, 'I will do this: I will pull down my barns and build larger ones, and there I will store all my grain and my goods. And I will say to my soul, Soul, you have ample goods laid up for many years; relax, eat, drink, be merry.' But God said to him, 'You fool! This very night your life is being demanded of you. And the things you have prepared, whose will they be?'" (see Luke 12:16–20).

James showed how evil thoughts lead to prejudice and discrimination, saying, "For if a person with gold rings and in fine clothes comes into your assembly, and if a poor person in dirty clothes also comes in, and if you take notice of the one wearing the fine clothes and say, 'Have a seat here, please,' while to the one who is poor you say, 'Stand there,' or, 'Sit at my feet,' have you not made distinctions among yourselves, and become judges with evil thoughts?" (see James 2:2–4). Hatred, lust, greed, and prejudice cause most of our problems, but they are all things that can be hidden. Scripture says, "The heart is devious above all else; it is perverse" (Jer 17:9).

Some thoughts are not necessarily evil; they are just negative. Those that are filled with worry and dread are unproductive and harmful. Jesus warned against preoccupation with material things. Some thoughts are simply futile. Obsessing about things you cannot change is useless. Idle thoughts are a waste of time. Idle thoughts include guilt about the past and anxiety about the future. Regretting what we said or did doesn't solve problems. Dreading what might happen doesn't prevent problems. If only and What if? are wasted phrases!

Too many people are careless in regard to thoughts. Moral individuals who are extremely careful to guard their words and control their actions can be remarkably careless about their thoughts. They seem to believe that as long as an idea or belief is not expressed in audible words or visible deeds, it's of no consequence. They imagine that since no one hears or sees or knows about the bad thoughts that occupy their minds, then these thoughts are harmless. That's not true! We wouldn't put water in our gas tank or broken glass in our food, but we put evil, negative, and idle thoughts in our mind.

Furthermore, the longer we hold evil, negative, and idle thoughts, the more damage they will do and the harder they will be to remove. In fact, if we think evil, negative, and unproductive thoughts, we'll actually become evil, negative, and unproductive. On the other hand, if we think good, positive, and productive thoughts, we'll become good, positive, and productive. Solomon said, "As he thinketh in his heart, so is he" (Prov 23:7, KJV). Our thinking patterns must also be consistent. Once when his disciples were hesitant, Jesus said, "Why do doubts arise in your hearts?" (Luke 24:38).

If we think good thoughts in church and evil thoughts at work, we are deceitful. If we think positive thoughts at one o'clock and negative thoughts at two o'clock, we nullify the principle of returns. If we think productive thoughts when we're with certain people and idle thoughts when we're with other people, we're caught in a dangerous conflict.

Even so, actively fighting against such unwanted thoughts won't work. Jesus knew that the more we try to attack a thing, the more insidious it becomes. Thoughts are remarkably stubborn. If someone tells you not to think about purple rabbits, that's all you'll be able to do!

Also, much evil is caused by ignorance, and punishment is useless for solving that problem. Hitting a child certainly won't help him learn to spell words correctly. Instead, we must change our habits. We must substitute other thoughts. We must get busy on worthy projects. We must interact with wise, mature people.

The scriptures give a list of the best thoughts: "Whatever is true, whatever is honorable, whatever is just, whatever is pure, whatever is pleasing, whatever is commendable, if there is any excellence and if there is anything worthy of praise, think about these things" (Phil 4:8).

Remember, God knows our thoughts. Even though thoughts are invisible, they are still real and will be judged. Understanding how Jesus thought and how he stressed the importance of thinking will help us know him better and become more like him.

The remains of this small first-century synagogue are in Magdala, the hometown of Mary Magdalene. Located on the shore of the Sea of Galilee and just a few miles west of Capernaum, it's a likely location for Jesus to have taught when he "went throughout Galilee, teaching in their synagogues and proclaiming the good news of the kingdom" (Matthew 4:23).
—*Photo copyright Tony Cartledge*

Chapter 4

Jesus Spoke Wise Words

Jesus's sermons, parables, and even his conversations reveal his temperament and his ideas. They prove that he felt very strongly about certain issues. He had a focused agenda and a few pet peeves. His teachings tell us what he considered important. He was determined to share his insights and disseminate crucial information. His last command to his disciples was clear: "Go therefore and make disciples of all nations… teaching them to obey everything that I have commanded you" (Matt 28:19–20). Most of the lessons he presented were about how to develop integrity of character, how to maintain harmonious relationships, and how to increase spirituality.

Jesus taught that good character must be based on a foundation of honesty and truth. He condemned self-righteousness. Over and over, Jesus repeated, "All who exalt themselves will be humbled, and those who humble themselves will be exalted" (Luke 14:11). Jesus despised hypocrisy. He ridiculed sanctimonious displays of righteousness (see Matt 6:2, 5–6; 23:2–3, 5–7, 23–25, 27–28).

Jesus also knew that wealth and possessions can give a false sense of security. Zacchaeus had problems with greed. The rich young ruler rejected Jesus's invitation and walked away because of greed. In fact, one of Jesus's most startling statements is about greed: "It is easier for a camel to go through the eye of a needle than for someone who is rich to enter the kingdom of God" (Matt 19:24).

Jesus warned against covetousness, and he emphasized perseverance as an essential character trait: "The one who endures to the end will be saved" (Matt 10:22; see also Luke 11:8). He stressed concern for others, saying, "I give you a new commandment, that you love one another. Just as I have loved you, you also should love one another" (John 13:34). He always supported the underdog and took the side of the outcast. He associated with the poor, the handicapped, the alienated, and especially with those who were different and considered "sinful." In fact, the famous "good Samaritan" is called good simply because he was the one who noticed and cared for the injured man. Scripture encourages generosity, saying, "God loves a cheerful giver" (2 Cor 9:7).

Surprisingly, Jesus ranked relationships as more important than worship, saying, "When you are offering your gift at the altar, if you remember that your brother or sister has something against you, leave your gift there before the altar and go; first be reconciled to your brother or sister, and then come and offer your gift" (Matt 5:23–24).

Forgiveness is essential in social relationships. Jesus gave a wonderful analogy about two debtors. One was forgiven a huge debt and then immediately persecuted a poor man who owed him a small debt. This caused the first lender to withdraw his favor and hand him over to the torturers. Then Jesus explained, "So my heavenly Father will also do to every one of you, if you do not forgive your brother or sister from your heart" (Matt 18:35).

When Peter asked, "'Lord, if another member of the church sins against me, how often should I forgive? As many as seven times?' Jesus said to him, 'Not seven times, but, I tell you, seventy-seven times'" (Matt 18:21–22). In other words, always forgive! Jesus certainly walked his talk concerning forgiveness by speaking from the cross about his executioners, saying, "Father, forgive them; for they do not know what they are doing" (Luke 23:34).

Jesus taught the value of service. In fact, he divided the population into goats and sheep, based upon the service they had rendered (see Matt 25:41–46). Jesus believed even little acts of service matter, saying, "Whoever gives even a cup of cold water…none of these will lose their reward" (Matt 10:42).

In his teachings on spirituality, Jesus insisted that people must get their priorities straight: "Strive first for the kingdom of God and his righteousness, and all these things will be given to you as well" (Matt 6:33). Then he told a parable, saying, "The kingdom of heaven is like treasure hidden in a field, which someone found and hid; then in his joy he goes and sells all that he has and buys that field…. The kingdom of heaven is like a merchant in search of fine pearls; on finding one pearl of great value, he went and sold all that he had and bought it" (Matt 13:44–46).

Jesus constantly stressed commitment to God. His first recorded words included, "Did you not know that I must be in my Father's house?" (Luke 2:49). Among his last words were, "Father, into your hands I commend my spirit" (Luke 23:46). He promised that faithfulness will be rewarded.

Jesus emphasized God's love for individuals. In one of his classic trilogies—the coin, the sheep, and the prodigal son—God is the seeker, and in each case love wins. In the well-known parable of the prodigal, the father, who represents God, gives his son freedom to leave and make his own foolish mistakes, but he continues to love him and immediately accepts him back without any recompense or punishment. That's grace!

This same concept is stated in the most frequently quoted Bible verse: "For God so loved the world that he gave his only Son, so that everyone who believes in him may not perish but may have eternal life" (John 3:16).

Jesus's teachings and words all center on three things: developing our own character; loving, forgiving, and serving others; and being faithful to God. Discovering what Jesus considered important and understanding what he emphasized through his words helps us know him better and become more like him.

Chapter 5

Jesus Performed Good Deeds

Jesus was an active, multitalented person. He spent his early adult years as a blue-collar worker in the carpenter trade. Later, he used his knowledge of construction in parables about the houses with either sand or rock foundations and about estimating the cost of a tower.

After the age of thirty, Jesus spent the rest of his life carrying out his mission to serve others. He dedicated his life to accomplishing God's purpose. Peter summed it up, saying, "[Jesus] went about doing good" (Acts 10:38). That "good" included his many teachings, stories, and conversations about concern for others, along with his many deeds and acts of service.

When Jesus's cousin John the Baptist was imprisoned, he sent a plea for reassurance. Strangely enough, Jesus didn't answer "yes" or "no." He didn't even quote scriptures to prove his identity. Instead, he gave evidence, and that evidence was, "I'm helping people." In a world with little medical knowledge and few pain-relieving measures, there was much suffering. Jesus seemed to be constantly alleviating discomfort and promoting healing. He helped some with physical problems. One woman spent all her money on doctors and had only gotten worse. Jesus declared that her faith made her well (see Mark 5:34).

Another woman was crippled, and Jesus healed her (see Luke 13:12–13). Some were blind (see Mark 10:46–47, 51–52). Jesus helped others with mental problems. We now know that chemical imbalances and brain disorders can cause people to act in destructive ways. In early days these unknown aberrations were called "demons." Jesus set them free (Matt 9:32–33).

Jesus also helped many with emotional healing. He knew that health issues can be caused by guilt and shame. Now, we don't know all of the details of these healings. Sometimes Jesus used touch (see Matt 8:15); sometimes he used clay (see John 9:6); sometimes he sent the patient to a priest (see Mark 1:44). But we do know that Jesus almost always said, "Your faith has made you well" (see Matt 9:22).

Research has proved that positive thinking is powerful. We also know that the ability to heal is still available to us because Jesus said, "The one who believes in me will also do the works that I do and, in fact, will do greater works than these" (John 14:12). Research experts, nurses, doctors, and surgeons perform great healing ministries every day. The only difference is that we use medical terms to describe them.

Besides healing, Jesus also fed the hungry, and he was even willing to do menial tasks. Since people wore sandals and walked on dusty roads, a servant usually washed guests' feet. But on one occasion Jesus himself did this job (see John 13:4–5).

Jesus comforted the sorrowful. In fact, he offered a general invitation, saying, "Come to me, all you that are weary and are carrying heavy burdens, and I will give you rest" (Matt 11:28).

Besides teaching, healing, feeding and comforting people, Jesus made many changes that disturbed the religious establishment, breaking long-standing rules and regulations. He made a momentous statement, declaring, "The sabbath was made for humankind, and not humankind for the sabbath" (Mark 2:27). In other words, the day of rest was established for the benefit of the people. People were not created for the purpose of keeping the proper rituals on the day of rest.

When Jesus healed on the sabbath, the critics objected. One incident shows how strict and illogical the rules were:

> At that time Jesus went through the grainfields on the sabbath; his disciples were hungry, and they began to pluck heads of grain and to eat. When the Pharisees saw it, they said to him, "Look, your disciples are doing what is not lawful to do on the sabbath." He said to them, "Have you not read what David did when he and his companions were hungry? He entered the house of God and ate the bread of the Presence, which it was not lawful for him or his companions to eat, but only for the priests. Or have you not read in the law that on the sabbath the priests in the temple break the sabbath and yet are guiltless?" (see Matt 12:1–5)

Jesus also changed many traditional beliefs and customs. He interacted with women, even sinful women like the woman at the well. He associated with prostitutes, inciting the Pharisees' anger. Jesus rebuked the Pharisees, saying, "Her sins, which were many, have been forgiven; hence she has shown great love" (see Luke 7:47).

In Jesus's culture, eating with someone indicated acceptance and social equality. That's why the Pharisees often asked, "Why does he eat with…sinners?" (see Mark 2:16).

He held discussions with Mary and defended her when Martha tried to make her do "women's work," saying, "Martha, Martha, you are worried and distracted by many things; there is need of only one thing. Mary has chosen the better part, which will not be taken away from her" (Luke 10:41–42).

He complimented a Roman centurion, who was considered an enemy and a heretic because soldiers were required to sacrifice to Caesar. Yet Jesus said, "In no one in Israel have I found such faith" (Matt 8:10).

He called a hated outcast Samaritan "a [good] neighbor" (see Luke 10:36). He told another parable about healing the ten lepers, and it was only the Samaritan who expressed appreciation" (see Luke 17:15–16).

He staged a public protest for justice when the money changers were cheating the people. The scriptures say, "[He] began to drive out those who were selling and those who were buying in the temple" (Mark 11:15).

Over and over, Jesus surprised and disturbed the political and religious leaders. Even his disciples were dumbfounded and appalled when Jesus said, "'It is easier for a camel to go through the eye of a needle than for someone who is rich to enter the kingdom of God.' When the disciples heard this, they were greatly astounded and said, 'Then who can be saved?'" (Matt 19:24–25).

Jesus was definitely a people person. He socialized with his disciples, with friends, and even with those who were shunned by proper society. His first miracle was at a wedding reception. He often had dinner and fellowship with individuals, including Zacchaeus and Mary, Martha and Lazarus. He also described a party with food, music, and dancing to honor the return of the prodigal son.

Jesus honored children. One day, "he took a little child and put it among them; and taking it in his arms, he said to them, 'Whoever welcomes one such child in my name welcomes me'" (Mark 9:36–37). He held and blessed the children (see Mark 10:13–16).

It's obvious that Jesus was active and busy, but he wasn't a "workaholic." Instead, he insisted upon downtime and spent many hours in reflection and meditation. He was alone for forty days after his baptism, probably praying and making plans for his future ministry (see Matt 4:1–2).

After a stressful period, Jesus told his disciples to "'come away to a deserted place all by yourselves and rest a while.' For many were coming and going, and they had no leisure even to eat. And they went away in the boat to a deserted place by themselves" (Mark 6:31–32). On another occasion the scripture says, "At daybreak he departed and went into a deserted place" (Luke 4:42). At times, "[Jesus] went out to the mountain to pray; and he spent the night in prayer to God" (Luke 6:12).

So we've seen that Jesus lived a productive, God-centered life. He balanced good works with social interaction and quiet times. Jesus taught, healed the sick, fed the hungry, comforted the brokenhearted, changed many rules and customs, and spent much time in personal thought and prayer. Understanding these details about Jesus's activities and achievements helps us to know him better and become more like him.

Chapter 6

Jesus Possessed Common Sense

Almost everyone knows that Jesus was the Messiah. They call him Lord and Savior. They appreciate his wonderful words and his benevolent deeds. They may even try to obey him and worship him. But Jesus has one unexpected attribute that's often ignored and overlooked. That attribute is his down-to-earth common sense. Jesus didn't walk around with his head in the clouds. He wasn't a pious moralist or a religious fanatic. Instead, he was a sensible man with touches of humor and even satire. From his youth Jesus felt a compelling call from God, saying, "My food is to do the will of him who sent me and to complete his work" (John 4:34).

He was practical rather than idealistic. He learned early in his ministry that his teachings and actions would not be accepted, even by his own family and friends. However, Jesus never sought popularity. He minimized miraculous signs and events, saying, "The kingdom of God is not coming with things that can be observed.... For, in fact, the kingdom of God is among you" (Luke 17:20–21).

Jesus didn't try to gather crowds or encourage notoriety. In fact, several times he urged his disciples to avoid publicity (see, e.g., Matt 8:4; 17:9; Mark 7:32, 34–36; 8:29–30; Luke 8:56). He tried to keep some things private because he knew hyped-up events and exciting fads don't last. He didn't want his message and ministry to be based on a few wonders and miracles. In both teachings and actions, Jesus preferred simplicity and honesty. He was skeptical about insincere speech, saying, "On the day of judgment you will have to give an account for every careless word you utter" (Matt 12:36).

In fact, Jesus often complained about empty words, and he avoided sanctimonious language. A woman said "Blessed is the womb that bore you and the breasts that nursed you!" Jesus denied this, saying, "Blessed rather are those who hear the word of God and obey it!" (Luke 11:27–28).

Instead of quoting platitudes or citing laws, Jesus used logic and analytical thinking. He told some critical Pharisees that "if one blind person guides another, both will fall into a pit" (Matt 15:14).

To encourage the acceptance of new ideas, he gave an example, saying, "No one sews a piece of unshrunk cloth on an old cloak; otherwise, the patch pulls away from it, the new from the old, and a worse tear is made. And no one puts new wine into old wineskins; otherwise, the wine will burst the skins, and the wine is lost, and so are the skins; but one puts new wine into fresh wineskins" (Mark 2:21–22).

Jesus knew that people tend to be stubborn and reluctant to change. In the parable of the rich man who begged Abraham to send a warning about punishment to his brothers, Jesus quoted Abraham: "If they do not listen to Moses and the prophets, neither will they be convinced even if someone rises from the dead" (Luke 16:31).

It may shock some people to discover that Jesus relied on hard evidence, rather than doctrinal purity or traditional orthodoxy, when judging people or faith systems. He said, "Every tree that does not bare good fruit is cut down and thrown into the fire. Thus you will know them by their fruits" (Matt 7:19–20). "Fruits" are the results or consequences of words and deeds. He is saying that if a belief or practice doesn't produce positive and helpful outcomes, then that belief or practice is false. If some rule or law causes harm to individuals, then that rule or law should be abolished.

Jesus gave instructions about handling conflicts, saying, "Come to terms quickly with your accuser while you are on the way to court with him, or your accuser may hand you over to the judge, and the judge to the guard, and you will be thrown into prison" (Matt 5:25–26). His conversation with the scribes and priests about a tax problem was reasonable (see Luke 20:24–25).

The parable about the reluctant judge reveals Jesus's grasp of human nature: "A widow…[came to a judge], saying, 'Grant me justice against my opponent.' For a while he refused; but later he said to himself, 'Though I have no fear of God and no respect for anyone, yet because this widow keeps bothering me, I will grant her justice, so that she may not wear me out by continually coming" (see Luke 18:2–5).

As a carpenter, he knew about financial pitfalls and advised careful planning: "For which of you, intending to build a tower, does not first sit down and estimate the cost, to see whether he has enough to complete it? Otherwise, when he has laid a foundation and is not able to finish, all who see it will begin to ridicule him, saying, 'This fellow began to build and was not able to finish'" (see Luke 14:28–30). Then he used a similar analogy about war, saying, "What king, going out to wage war against another king, will not sit down first and consider whether he is able with ten thousand to oppose the one who comes against him with twenty thousand? If he cannot, then, while the other is still far away, he sends a delegation and asks for the terms of peace" (Luke 14:31–32).

Jesus never expected his followers to be naive and gullible. Instead, when he sent out his disciples, his warning was blunt: "Be wise as serpents and innocent as doves" (Matt 10:16). To illustrate the importance of being alert and watchful, he reminded his listeners of an obvious principle, saying, "If the owner of the house had known in what part of the night the thief was coming, he would have stayed awake and would not have let his house be broken into" (Matt 24:43).

Jesus was sensible and cautious. He never took unnecessary risks. He didn't succumb to temptation when Satan dared him to jump off the temple spire. Later, he continued to be careful and discreet. When enemies were seeking him, he explained to his brothers why he would not join them for a celebration in Jerusalem (see John 7:6–9). He avoided unnecessary confrontations.

It's interesting to discover that Jesus was frugal; he didn't waste any resources (see Mark 8:8). He didn't waste effort on unproductive projects either (see Matt 7:6). Nor did he waste time on dead-end paths, adamantly demanding people to cut their losses and move on (Matt 10:14).

It's significant that the term hell actually comes from the word gehenna, which was the name of a well-known dump for waste material. This indicates that Jesus viewed evil as something to be eradicated, not necessarily punished.

Theology and morality are not the only subjects Jesus discussed. He loved nature and used it in many parables. He compared his evangelistic outreach to an everyday activity that ordinary people could understand, saying, "Follow me, and I will make you fish for people" (Matt 4:19). He used common plants to explain morals, saying, "You will know them by their fruits. Are grapes gathered from thorns, or figs from thistles?" (Matt 7:16). He enjoyed the beauty of flowers (see Matt 6:28–29). He talked about God's care of birds and other animals (see Matt 6:26; Luke 9:58).

Now, most people view Jesus as a religious icon instead of as a living, breathing human being. That's unfortunate, because, since we are human beings who have been told to follow his example, we need to be aware of his special interests and personal habits. These vignettes give us a deeper understanding of his common-sense approach to life. This will help us to know him better and become more like him.

Ruins of the original Capernaum synagogue in which
Jesus taught as recorded in Mark 1:21.
—*Photo copyright Tony Cartledge*

Chapter 7

Jesus Revealed the Nature of God

In the final hours of his life on earth, Jesus had an interesting conversation with Pilate. When the question of his identity and role was raised, Jesus clearly defined his purpose and mission, saying, "For this I was born, and for this I came into the world, to testify to the truth" (John 18:37).

If this is the case, then it is imperative for us to understand what truth he was seeking to reveal and what purpose he was seeking to accomplish. Regardless of some artistic depictions and some linguistic representations, Jesus wasn't a wild-eyed fanatic. He wasn't a weird ascetic. He wasn't a religious recluse. Instead, he was a strong, fascinating man who delivered a message of hope and lived a life of service.

Let's consider the great truth Jesus bore witness to concerning the nature of God. Jesus said, "Whoever sees me sees him who sent me" (John 12:45). Philip had raised this issue with a profound request, saying, "Lord, show us the Father, and we will be satisfied" (John 14:8). Jesus replied with a mind-blowing revelation, saying, "Have I been with you all this time, Philip, and you still do not know me? Whoever has seen me has seen the Father. How can you say, 'Show us the Father'?" (John 14:9).

The first thing Jesus taught is that God is spirit and we must worship him in spirit and in truth (see John 4:24). This is important, because it means God is not an external, tangible, visible object. Most religions of that time, and some even today, think of God as a person, place, or thing. These are idols. Instead, God is an indwelling presence.

There is no specific definition of Spirit in the scriptures. The term literally means "breath or air," which is an invisible force. It was the divine anointing of this Spirit that established Jesus's identity (see Matt 3:16–17). This was a symbolic description expressing the fact that Jesus sensed God's presence and approval. The Spirit was the powerful impetus that enabled Jesus to accomplish his mission of mercy. Jesus felt God's guidance and call to service.

Many scriptures indicate that God's spirit interacts with us. Jesus said, "The Spirit of truth…abides with you, and he will be in you" (John 14:17). The scriptures give us significant insight about our own position and role, saying, "Do you not know that you are God's temple and that God's Spirit dwells in you?" (1 Cor 3:16). Jesus assures us that the Spirit bestows wisdom, giving us knowledge and understanding.

The next attribute of God is that he is just. Jesus said, "Will not God grant justice to his chosen ones who cry to him day and night?" (Luke 18:7). Jesus describes his impartiality by showing that he doesn't favor any particular person or group (see Matt 5:45). He assures us of God's concern.

Scripture says God cares about us and our problems: "Cast all your anxiety on him, because he cares for you" (1 Pet 5:7). He explains that since God wants us to be with him, he seeks us when we stray. He told the story of the good shepherd looking for one lost lamb and of a woman looking for her lost coin, describing her joy when she found it (see Luke 15:4, 8).

In those days, most people's idea of God was negative and paganistic. They thought of him as a wrathful, vengeful creature, constantly judging, condemning, and punishing mankind for every mistake. Then Jesus arrived, giving people an entirely different view of God. He told Philip that he came to earth to live a life that reflected God's attributes.

In short, Jesus came to provide an accurate representation of God! We are able to see and understand the nature of God by observing the life of Jesus, and this view shows that he is loving, not punitive!

Jesus illustrates God's goodness by asking two simple questions: "Is there anyone among you who, if your child asks for a fish, will give a snake instead of a fish? Or if the child asks for an egg, will give a scorpion?" (Luke 11:11–12). Any honest person realizes that no father would do these things. Therefore, God does not do these things. Indeed, the scripture is succinct: "God is love" (1 John 4:8).

Another important attribute of God is that he's forgiving, not vengeful. His mercy is absolute. As such, Jesus extended forgiveness to Zacchaeus, to the woman at the well, to the woman caught in the act of adultery, and even to the soldiers who were carrying out the crucifixion.

Finally, Jesus reveals a God who offers us freedom, not slavery. God is omnipotent, but he never uses that power to force his will on anyone.

Jesus had a choice about his fate, but he prayed for God's will to be done. He allowed Judas to betray him. He allowed Peter to deny him. He allowed the other disciples to desert him. Jesus loved the rich young ruler, but he let him walk away. Jesus meant what he said: "You will know the truth, and the truth will make you free…. So if the Son makes you free, you will be free indeed" (John 8:32, 36).

In the parable of the talents, each man was allowed to do whatever he chose with his resources. The master didn't issue any specific orders to these men concerning the investment of their talents. He didn't stay there to impose his will on them about their talents. He didn't look over their shoulders and supervise their actions. Instead, the men with the talents were totally free to do what they wanted to do. He gave them independence. He let them decide whether to be responsible or irresponsible. He set them free.

The parable of the prodigal is a brief allegory of the gospel. In this story, Jesus explains how God treats his wayward children. He gave his son the freedom to make mistakes. He let him suffer the consequences of those mistakes. When he chose to return, the father welcomed him back with joy and grace.

It's important to note that the prodigal was God's son before, during, and after his rebellion. He never ceased to be God's son. God's children are promised a position of permanent security. Jesus said, "I give them eternal life, and they will never perish. No one will snatch them out of my hand. What my Father has given me is greater than all else, and no one can snatch it out of the Father's hand" (John 10:28–29).

Near the end of his life, Jesus prayed, "I glorified you on earth by finishing the work that you gave me to do" (John 17:4). The word glorify actually means to "make God look good." Jesus tells us that as Christians we're to "make God look good" with our lives: "Let your light shine before others, so that they may see your good works and give glory to your Father in heaven" (Matt 5:16). Furthermore, Jesus revealed that God wants us to be like him: "Be perfect, therefore, as your heavenly Father is perfect" (Matt 5:48).

It was Jesus's purpose to change the concept of God from physical (see Gen 3:8) to spiritual (see John 4:24). He showed us a God who is impartial and just. He is loving, not punitive. He is merciful, not vengeful. He gives blessings, not punishments. He offers freedom, not slavery. He allows us to make our own decisions, yet he seeks us when we stray.

God imparts wisdom and understanding. He will be with us forever. It was Jesus's purpose to move the idea of God from "out there" (see Exod 19:3) to "in here" (see John 14:17). God works through our conscience, our feelings, our thoughts, our words, our deeds, and our circumstances to enrich our lives. Most importantly, we've learned that God demonstrated all of these positive attributes through the personality, words, and deeds of Jesus Christ.

Knowing that "to reveal the nature of God" was a major purpose of Jesus's life helps us to know him better and become more like him.

Sunrise over the Sea of Galilee at Ginosar, also known as the Lake of Gennesaret. In Matthew's gospel account Jesus sailed across the Sea of Galilee, landing at the ancient town of Ginosar that was referred to as Kinneret in the Book of Joshua. At Ginosar a crowd gathered around Jesus, and many were cured.
—*Photo copyright Bruce Gourley*

Chapter 8

Jesus Explained the Problem of Evil

Jesus said, "I came to bear witness to the truth." Another one of those truths was to explain the problem of evil. When he discussed this subject, it's obvious that he was a realist. He told it like it was! He never sugar-coated situations. He warned his followers that evil is a real and present danger: "Blessed are you when people revile you and persecute you and utter all kinds of evil against you falsely on my account" (Matt 5:11).

He described humanity's weakness, criticizing groups who wouldn't listen to his teachings and insisted on miraculous demonstrations.

In a parable about the wheat and tares, he tells us how to deal with evil:

> The kingdom of heaven may be compared to someone who sowed good seed in his field; but while everybody was asleep, an enemy came and sowed weeds among the wheat, and then went away. So when the plants came up and bore grain, then the weeds appeared as well. And the slaves of the householder came and said to him, "Master, did you not sow good seed in your field? Where, then, did these weeds come from?" He answered, "An enemy

has done this." The slaves said to him, "Then do you want us to go and gather them?" But he replied, "No; for in gathering the weeds you would uproot the wheat along with them. Let both of them grow together until the harvest; and at harvest time I will tell the reapers, Collect the weeds first and bind them in bundles to be burned, but gather the wheat into my barn.'" (Matt 13:24–30)

Many well-meaning Christians are like these servants—anxious to go out and battle evil. But Jesus knew that we simply don't know enough to pull the weeds out of the wheat without damaging the wheat and doing more harm than good. Jesus knew that since we aren't omniscient, we can't see the whole picture. We can't understand all the implications of complex problems. We are not able to predict the future and see the final result of our decisions. Sometimes we can't even recognize the difference between wheat and weeds.

Many people who heard the parable about the publican and the Pharisee praying in the temple would have judged the hated publican, who cheated people on their taxes, to be a "weed" and the moral Pharisee, who tithed so conscientiously, to be "wheat," but they would be wrong. Many people would have judged Mary Magdalene, who had many personal problems, to be a "weed" and the rich young ruler, who kept all the commandments, to be "wheat," but they would be wrong. Jesus made that point when he told the chief priests and elders that "the tax collectors and the prostitutes are going into the kingdom of God ahead of you" (Matt 21:31).

It's easy for religious people to moralize, attack evil, and fight for what's right. It sounds good. It gets attention. It instigates crusades. But it's neither scriptural nor productive. Overreacting to evil can backfire. In our world of audio and video communication, even criticizing an issue can give it attention, actually strengthening and rewarding it. Furthermore, angry, name-calling, card-waving individuals are not particularly good witnesses for a God of love. One wise writer said, "The caring kindness of a heathen is more Christlike than the furious zeal of a Christian."

Judgmental Christians can cause more damage than the sins they judge. But compromising and tolerating evil isn't the answer either. It may keep us from being labeled as fanatics, but it's neither scriptural or productive. There's a time to confront and a time to cooperate, but for permanent progress we must be changemakers who pray, "Lord, send world reform, but let it begin in me."

Jesus told another parable about evil that has very pertinent warnings for us:

> When the unclean spirit has gone out of a person, it wanders through waterless regions looking for a resting place, but not finding any, it says, "I will return to my house from which I came." When it comes, it finds it swept and put in order. Then it goes and brings seven other spirits more evil than itself, and they enter and live there; and the last state of that person is worse than the first. (Luke 11:24–26)

This story reveals a profound principle: that nature abhors a vacuum. Human beings have to fill their time with something. If the brain isn't thinking productive thoughts, it will think unproductive thoughts. Likewise, if our mouths are not saying positive things, they will probably be saying negative things. Very few people are content to remain silent for long periods. In the same way, if our bodies are not doing constructive things, they will most likely be doing destructive things. People become restless if they aren't moving.

Therefore, if we have evil thoughts or harmful habits, we can't just quit having them. Instead, we must replace them with good thoughts and beneficial habits. If we don't do this, the old ones will come back with reinforcements, and we'll be worse off than we were before. As the scripture says, "Do not be overcome by evil, but overcome evil with good" (Rom 12:21).

We must not criticize or attack those things we consider to be evil until we have learned all the facts and prepared a positive replacement.

Too many individuals spend their time and resources fighting habits or behaviors or objects they consider evil. Too many religions spend their time and resources fighting doctrines or beliefs or practices they consider evil. Christians are often against so many things that no one really knows what they are for. Jesus wasn't like that!

In fact, Jesus didn't seem to be overly concerned about many of the well-known sins that fanatics today are so determined to eradicate. He didn't emphasize theft, promiscuity, or drunkenness. He didn't even mention several of the "social sins" that modern evangelists and moralists spend their time condemning. He knew that many of these flaws and faults may simply be the consequences of unmet needs or the result of normal human weaknesses. Instead, he dealt with the inner, unlabeled sins that are more insidious and entrenched, such as judgment, hypocrisy, and greed.

Current ideas about evil are quite different from Jesus's ideas. The hidden hatred that causes us to criticize and ridicule others is often excused and considered humorous. Hypocrisy is sometimes viewed as an essential skill that enables us to be popular, have successful job interviews, and win elections. Lust, envy, and pride are not on most people's lists of sins. Greed that causes us to be selfish and neglectful of others is not a crime; sometimes it is praised as good business sense. Yet Jesus knew that these evils, which can be dormant within each of us, eventually will emerge and cause great damage.

When the Pharisees complained about certain forbidden foods and drinks, Jesus redirected their criticism: "It is not what goes into the mouth that defiles a person, but it is what comes out of the mouth that defiles" (Matt 15:11). He admitted that he was not a strict follower of all the rules and regulations, saying, "For John came neither eating nor drinking, and they say, 'He has a demon'; the Son of Man came eating and drinking, and they say, 'Look, a glutton and a drunkard, a friend of tax collectors and sinners!'" (Matt 11:18–19).

The scriptures also point out that it's not the specific things or actions themselves that are evil. It's the way they are used that causes problems. In other words, a glass of wine or a marijuana plant is not evil in and of itself. Instead, it's the addiction or the irresponsible human behavior or the loss of Christian witness they may cause that can result in evil. In the past, Christian groups forbade dancing because it was associated with rowdy behavior and drunken brawls on the Western frontier. But Jesus said there was dancing at the party celebrating the return of the prodigal son. Again, the specific activity wasn't harmful, but rather the places and things it was associated with.

Furthermore, the scriptures remind us that even a small evil thought or word or deed can grow into a huge problem (e.g., 1 Cor 5:6). A small amount of poison can contaminate an entire water supply. A few cholera germs can infect a whole population. Too often, when people make questionable decisions or cut corners or push the envelope, they justify their actions by saying, "This one little false word or this one little wrong deed won't make any difference." But Scripture says, "One bungler destroys much good" (Eccl 9:18).

Jesus always evaluated sin and evil by the law of love. He broke sabbath laws to help hurting people. He changed traditions and customs to include outsiders and misfits. He "rocked the boat" and even scattered the money and upset the tables of deceitful merchants to keep them from cheating worshipers.

Paul applied this law of love when he explained his personal moral code: "Do not, for the sake of food, destroy the work of God. Everything is indeed clean, but it is wrong for you to make others fall by what you eat; it is good not to eat meat or drink wine or do anything that makes your brother or sister stumble" (Rom 14:20–21). Paul also said, "To the pure all things are pure, but to the corrupt and unbelieving nothing is pure" (Titus 1:15).

Jesus included evil as one of the truths he came to define because he knew it was a powerful and deadly enemy of mankind. He also knew it was difficult to deal with because wheat and tares look so much alike. Evil includes negative and idle thoughts, critical and hurtful words, vicious and destructive deeds. It includes careless mistakes and poor choices. It includes anything done with deceitful or selfish motives or anything that has unproductive consequences.

Understanding Jesus's viewpoint about determining what is evil and following his advice about the best methods for handling it will enable us to know him better and to be more like him!

Matthew, Mark and Luke record Jesus' baptism in the Jordan River north of the Dead Sea. In this image brush lines the bank of the Jordan River near where Jesus was baptized, on the present-day border with the nation of Jordan.
—*Photo copyright Bruce Gourley*

Chapter 9

Jesus Promised the Possibility of Redemption

Jesus said he came to bear witness to the truth, one of which included the possibility of redemption. Sins can be forgiven; lives can be changed; people can start over with a clean slate. In a well-known encounter, Jesus dealt with a moral, intelligent, educated religious leader named Nicodemus. During an intimate, late-night discussion, this momentous life change was described as a "new birth." Jesus said, "No one can enter the kingdom of God without being born of water and Spirit" (John 3:5), referring to a statement from the Old Testament (see Ezek 36:25–27). Jesus's explanation to Nicodemus about redemption became the most famous verse in the Bible: "For God so loved the world that he gave his only Son, so that everyone who believes in him may not perish but may have eternal life" (John 3:16).

It's encouraging to learn that Jesus enabled many men and women to take advantage of this promise. The woman at the well had five husbands and a live-in lover, but she became a missionary. Zacchaeus was a traitor and a cheater, but he turned his life around. The demoniac was so violent that he had to be chained, but Jesus sent him home to teach others. Peter cursed, lied, and denied Jesus, but he still preached to thousands. Paul was a murderer who tried to kill Christians and destroy the church, but he wrote much of the New Testament. The thief on the cross was a hardened criminal who asked for mercy and was rewarded with paradise. These prove that redemption is possible!

Over and over, Jesus said, "Don't judge, and don't condemn." Over and over, Jesus forgave and redeemed sinners. Over and over, Jesus offered hope and a new life. He summed up the matter in one sentence: "God did not send the Son into the world to condemn the world, but in order that the world might be saved through him" (John 3:17).

So what is redemption? To redeem really means to salvage or ransom. The scripture says, "They are now justified by his grace as a gift, through the redemption that is in Christ Jesus" (Rom 3:24). But what happens in people's hearts and minds that enables them to change? In short, how is the wonderful miracle of redemption accomplished? Well, the dramatic transformation of attitudes and behavior occurs because salvation fills the person's deepest needs.

God knows we have needs. Furthermore, God wants to fulfill those needs. When our needs are met, we no longer have to practice harmful habits or perform destructive actions in a desperate search for fulfillment.

Of course all of us have physical needs—such as air, food, water, clothes, and shelter—but we also have mental and emotional needs. One of our basic needs is acceptance. No one wants to be rejected or shunned or turned away. In their vain efforts to be accepted, young people are often tempted to join cults or gangs or undesirable social groups. This need to belong or urge to fit in is such a powerful draw that even adult men and women will compromise their morals, lower their standards, and engage in destructive behavior.

But such compromises are unnecessary, for Jesus assures us of acceptance. We don't have to feel abandoned when friends leave us. We don't have to feel betrayed when associates fail to support us. We don't have feel helpless or fearful when adversaries oppose us. Redemption assures us that we are accepted!

The next thing we all need is a sense of value. No one wants to feel worthless or insignificant. It's a relief to finally realize that our life does have significance. We don't have to look for fame and fortune in all the wrong places. We don't have to boast or brag in order to prove our worth. We don't have to bully others in order to feel important. Redemption assures us that we are valuable!

Additionally, we all need to feel forgiven. No one wants to live with overwhelming feelings of guilt and shame. All of us have made choices we wish we could change. All of us have said words we would like to unsay. All of us have done things we would like to undo. But words can't be unsaid, and deeds can't be undone. Nevertheless, with forgiveness, regret is abolished. We know that God can remove our sin and even help us use those bad decisions and destructive actions for good as we learn from our mistakes. We don't have to dread a day of judgment or expect eternal punishment. Redemption assures us that we are forgiven!

The need for security is also universal. No one can live happily and productively with constant feelings of worry and uncertainty. Jesus knew this, which is why he repeated the words fear not so many times. There are a lot of dangers in this world. Disease, crime, terrorism, drugs, painful relationships, and financial problems are rampant. But redemption assures us that we are secure!

The final thing we all need is a sense of purpose. No one wants to live an empty, futile, useless life. So many people are confused and discontented. They change college majors, career choices, and life partners. They move from job to job and city to city searching for meaning and fulfillment.

We need to find our niche. We need to choose occupations, volunteer activities, and recreation outlets that use our strengths, avoid our weaknesses, and give us satisfaction. We need to have productive goals. We need to succeed and accomplish those goals. In addition to this, as Christians, we have the overriding mission to constantly represent God and help to bring in his kingdom. Redemption assures us that we have a purpose in life!

The only thing an individual has to do in order to receive and benefit from this wonderful gift of redemption is to believe that such a change is possible—to believe that God will keep his promise and do what he says he will do. This belief leads to a transformation called conversion.

Jesus realized that all kinds of people would hear his message. He also realized they would respond in different ways, which he addresses in the parable of the sower. The "seed" is the gospel message. When it "falls by the wayside," that means the people who hear it have no background, no preparation, and no interest in changing their lives. They disregard or ridicule the scriptural quotes or sermons or Christian witnesses.

The seeds that fall in shallow ground are received by those who are eager to listen to anything new. They will probably respond and quickly begin to practice some form of religion, but they have no depth, and their enthusiasm soon fades. These are the dropouts, who fill our church rolls but not our pews.

The seeds that fall among thorns are received by those who may have a sincere desire to change, but because they lack a support group or face a lot of opposition, they will likely give up.

The seeds that fall on good ground are received by those "few who find the narrow way." These individuals experience a true conversion, and they last for the long haul. Some produce a lot of fruit, and others produce a little fruit, but they are the ones who keep our churches alive and provide the "salt and light" for the world.

Yes, many different people hear the message of redemption. Some fall by the wayside; some quickly wither; some are choked by thorns; and some become productive. Which will we be?

The people who represent the good soil that will produce good fruits are those who are honestly committed to making Jesus's teachings the guiding principles of their lives. These "redeemed" ones have several spiritual characteristics: Because they know they are accepted, they will be able to accept others; they will avoid prejudice, pride, and discrimination. Because they know they have value, they will value others; they will treat other people with respect, avoiding harming or demeaning or bullying people by words or deeds. Because they know they are forgiven, they can forgive others; they won't hold grudges or become bitter; they won't retaliate or wreak vengeance. Because they know they are secure, they will be concerned about others; they will be generous and helpful and devoted to service. Because they know they have a purpose, they will be productive and successful at whatever they do; they won't get involved in selfish enterprises; instead, they will try to make the world a better place and bring in the kingdom of God.

The possibility of redemption gives us the opportunity to leave the past behind and begin a new life. It enables us to love as Jesus loved and live as Jesus lived, which helps us to know him better and to be more like him.

Chapter 10

Jesus Stressed the Importance of Concern

Jesus said, "I came to bear witness to the truth," one of which included the importance of concern for others. Nothing was more evident in Jesus's life than his genuine concern for those around him. From lepers to prostitutes, from foreigners to criminals, he reached out to ease their pain and fill their needs.

In fact, Jesus said the true test of Christianity is our concern for people. He did not say, "All people will know you are my disciples if you memorize scriptures, believe the correct doctrines, or attend the synagogue regularly." Instead, he said, "By this everyone will know that you are my disciples, if you have love for one another" (John 13:35). While earlier prophets had talked of love, Jesus totally revolutionized this concept, saying, "You have heard that it was said, 'You shall love your neighbor and hate your enemy.' But I say to you, love your enemies and pray for those who persecute you" (Matt 5:43–44).

When asked which was the most important commandment, instead of mentioning murder, adultery, or theft, Jesus talked about loving God and loving one's neighbor (see Matt 22:37–39). If those two are kept, then the others will be kept as well.

All of Jesus's activities were motivated by concern. He had little interest in fame and fortune, and he strove to eradicate self-righteousness. When the mob wanted to obey the law and stone the adulteress, Jesus said, "Let anyone among you who is without sin be the first to throw a stone at her" (John 8:7). Of course, no one did!

Jesus summarized the ultimate definition of concern: "No one has greater love than this, to lay down one's life for one's friends" (John 15:13). Consider his relationship with Simon Peter, who was certainly not a perfect individual. He had great virtues and great vices. In short, he was a typical human being. At times he was praised. At other times he was reprimanded.

After Jesus's arrest, Peter denied knowing him—three times. However, Jesus showed true concern for Peter by forgiving him instead of condemning him, allowing Peter to state his love and devotion three times. Then he gave him an important assignment to show that his trust was restored: "Feed my sheep" (John 21:17).

Two brothers, James and John, were in Jesus's inner circle, but they too had several human faults. Jesus didn't berate them. Instead, he gave them playful nicknames, calling them Boanerges, which means "Sons of Thunder" (see Mark 3:17). These men were high-tempered and overly ambitious. Once, their mother requested certain high positions for them. Instead of scolding her for pride or greed, Jesus patiently explained that such a thing was impossible (see Matt 20:23).

Another disciple, Thomas, is known for his doubts, but we often forget his courage and devotion. When Jesus was about to enter an area of danger, Thomas was quick to say, "Let us also go, that we may die with him" (John 11:16). After the crucifixion, however, Thomas needed reassurance. Later, when the two met, Jesus didn't reject Thomas for his doubts; instead, he alleviated them.

Jesus often visited with one special family. The scripture says, "Jesus loved Martha and her sister and Lazarus" (John 11:5). Martha was the ideal homemaker. Jesus ate at her table and enjoyed her hospitality. But when she attacked Mary for shirking her duty as a woman, Jesus corrected her. Mary broke the rigid mold concerning a "woman's place."

In a time when women were allowed few roles in society, Jesus supported her choice to learn and discuss important matters (see Luke 10:38–42).

When women broke other traditions, Jesus always defended them. For example, Mary Magdalene was a woman with a past. She seems to have had many personal problems, yet she was also one of the few present at the crucifixion. Additionally, she was one of the first to see Jesus after the resurrection and was chosen to give the first gospel message (see Matt 28:1, 5, 7).

Jesus showed concern for all of these individuals and many more. The first step in showing concern is to simply notice the problem. The good Samaritan noticed the injured man. The rich miser, who ended up in Hades, didn't notice the poor, sick beggar at his doorway (see Luke 16:19–21, 25).

In today's busy, largely urban world, it's easy to overlook or avoid the many hurting people around us. It's also difficult to separate those with legitimate needs from those who are merely part of a scam. Thousands of con artists try to manipulate us by using false information to evoke sympathy. This causes many caring people to hesitate before responding to pleas for help.

After noticing the need and finding out if it is real, the next step in showing concern is deciding what kind of help is best. Some starving people need to be "given fish" immediately, but most people need the more long-term assistance of being taught "how to fish" so they can become self-supporting and independent.

Then we must determine the level of help that's needed. Some people's needs are so great that they will require long-term assistance. Some will only require temporary aid, and some can best be served by receiving a little information and encouragement.

Furthermore, we can't simply copy Jesus's forms of service, because society is drastically different today. Two thousand years ago, government assistance and charitable organizations weren't really in existence. Now, numerous programs and groups provide food, clothing, and other essentials for those in need. Incidentally, most of these philanthropic endeavors have been established as a result of Jesus's emphasis on concern.

The kind of concern Jesus advocated for was a way of life, not a casual financial handout or an occasional benevolent act. There are many ways to show concern. Attitudes, words, and actions can all show concern. Even our facial expressions, our tone of voice, and our body language can express concern.

In an alienated population, without much family time or many intimate encounters, people are yearning for personal attention. We don't have neighborly drop-ins or over-the-back-fence conversations today. Technology has replaced much human interaction. That's why a smile, a nod, or a touch can be so significant. Jesus noticed and praised the widow's donation. He reached out to touch and hold and encourage little children and was always available to hurting people. We must find ways to do that. A listening ear can be greatly appreciated. Lonely people are legion. There are many latchkey children, homebound senior citizens, elderly invalids and nursing home residents. Spending even a few moments with these people is important.

Jesus heard people's complaints and problems. He often asked, "What can I do for you?" We must find time to do that. A word of praise or a well-deserved compliment can be more important than writing a check to a charitable organization or endowing an institution. Everybody likes to hear "thank you." Everybody likes to receive a note of appreciation. Everybody yearns for a compliment. Saying "I'm grateful for the work you do" to an employee or mentioning "Your beautiful roses brighten my day" to a neighbor costs nothing and is worth so much. Jesus wasn't reluctant to express his love to people.

Furthermore, even "gossip" can be used in a helpful way. Most people seem eager to pass on tidbits of information. Fortunately, there is a way to do so productively. Concerned Christians can make it a practice always to "pass on" any bit of good news, positive comment, or favorable statement that one individual mentions about another person. Even more importantly, concerned Christians can make it a practice never to "pass on" any bit of bad news, negative comment, or critical statement that one individual mentions about another person. Passing on the good and ignoring the bad is a simple habit, but it's one that can make a real difference in the social climate.

Concern is a crucial element of Christianity. It defines Jesus's outlook and outreach, and it reflects our own purpose as Christians. Understanding and applying this characteristic helps us to know Jesus better and to become more like him!

Chapter 11

Jesus Encouraged the Acceptance of Responsibility

Jesus said, "I came to bear witness to the truth," one of which was to encourage the acceptance of responsibility. This is an issue that affects every single individual on earth. It has created an entirely new worldview. It has revolutionized life as we know it. Up until the time of Jesus, almost every man, woman, and child had occupied either a master or a slave position, either a king or a subject role. This means a few dictators ruled and everyone else was subservient.

That's why it was both remarkable and controversial when Jesus raised ordinary men and women to a new level of equality, autonomy, and authority. He dared to say, "You are my friends if you do what I command you. I do not call you servants any longer, because the servant does not know what the master is doing; but I have called you friends, because I have made known to you everything that I have heard from my Father" (John 15:14–15). Over and over, he taught that as believers we are not lowly creatures. We are not unworthy sinners. We are not second-class citizens. We are not simply obedient subordinates; we are children of God.

In fact, Jesus went further than that. He insisted that, as Christians, we actually have the same relationship to God that he has. Later, Paul made the same awesome declaration, indicating that human beings can have such a relationship with Jesus. Scripture says, "For the one who sanctifies and those who are sanctified all have one Father. For this reason Jesus is not ashamed to call them brothers and sisters" (Heb 2:11).

Along with equality, Jesus also gave us autonomy, and he expects us to use our independence productively. He said we have the same right to approach and petition the Father as he does. Jesus denounced irresponsibility. None of us should merely take up space and waste our time upon this earth. Each one of us can do something! It's astonishing to discover that Jesus's greatest condemnation was for those who committed the sin of neglect.

When the man with one talent made excuses for not investing it, the master said, "Take the talent from him, and give it to the one with the ten talents.... As for this worthless slave, throw him into the outer darkness, where there will be weeping and gnashing of teeth" (Matt 25:28, 30). Notice that this man didn't steal that money. He didn't lose that money. He didn't spend that money on himself. He didn't even make a bad investment. He just did nothing. That was his sin!

When the bridesmaids who neglected their lamps allowed them to go out, the scripture says, "When the foolish took their lamps, they took no oil with them" (Matt 25:3). When they did finally buy more oil, it was too late. The door was shut, and the bridegroom said, "I do not know you" (Matt 25:12). These five virgins were not denied access to the kingdom because of something terrible they had done. Instead, they were denied access to the kingdom because of something important they had left undone (see Matt 25:32–46).

The rich man who ignored the beggar Lazarus did not end up in torment because of crimes against his fellow man. He ended up in torment because he had neglected his fellow man (see Luke 16:19–25).

The priest and Levite who "passed by on the other side" of the injured victim were not condemned because they hurt the man, but rather because they failed to help the man (see Luke:10:30–37).

The individuals identified as goats rather than sheep were not sent into eternal punishment because they were great sinners, but because they had not ministered to the needy (see Matt 25:32–33).

Jesus spent much more time denouncing people for the good deeds they had not performed than he did denouncing people for the bad deeds they had performed. In other words, sins of omission may actually be more destructive than sins of commission.

As Christians, we have also been given great authority. Jesus declared that we are called to serve just as he was called to serve. He believed we are capable of bringing in the kingdom. In essence, Jesus gives each of us this assignment: "I'm leaving you here to walk in the world for me." Later, Paul simply said, "We are ambassadors for Christ" (2 Cor 5:20).

One of the most surprising descriptions concerning the status of believers is expressed in a scripture that says Jesus "hath made us kings and priests" (Rev 1:6, KJV). Later, another scripture says, "You have made them to be a kingdom and priests serving our God, and they will reign on earth" (Rev 5:10).

At that time priests and kings represented the highest ranks of power. Therefore, these designations about men and women are significant. But with privilege comes responsibility. Because of our position of authority, we're expected to use what we have and be good stewards of our resources.

Jesus's hope for the future depended upon his followers passing on his message. Furthermore, he warned us that we must not avoid this responsibility. We must not deny that we have a light. We must not hide or diminish our light. Salvation puts the light of God into believers. Jesus expects them to allow that light to shine on everyone they meet. In fact, Jesus's final verbal message was a divine commission: "You will be my witnesses in Jerusalem…and to the ends of the earth" (Acts 1:8).

Notice that there is no real choice about this matter. If we are Christians, then we are witnesses. We may be a bad witness or a mediocre witness or a good witness, but we will be a witness. That's because the world is constantly evaluating us as representatives of our heavenly Father.

Being a special spiritual emissary is a serious matter. Jesus pointed out a widow's offering as an example: "This poor widow has put in more than all those who are contributing to the treasury. For all of them have contributed out of their abundance; but she out of her poverty has put in everything she had, all she had to live on" (see Mark 12:43–44). This woman's generosity illustrates that God does not have one standard of stewardship for everyone. Instead, each person's service will be judged based on the amount of possessions and abilities that they have at their disposal.

Jesus is reasonable. He doesn't expect individuals to be what they can't be. He doesn't expect individuals to do what they can't do. He doesn't expect individuals to give what they don't have. Instead, each of us must use our own special abilities, talents, and skills. Each of us must pass on our own personal insights, knowledge, and wisdom. Each of us must use all of the resources that are available to us.

When Peter and John were approached by a beggar who expected them to give him some money, Peter said, "I have no silver or gold, but what I have I give you; in the name of Jesus Christ of Nazareth, stand up and walk" (Acts 3:6). We can respond similarly. We may not have much money, but we can give time. We may not have many possessions, but we can give encouragement. We may not have much talent, but we can give love. "Such as we have" we can and must provide.

All believers are accountable, but more is expected of some people than of others. Jesus explained this double standard with an illustration about servants: "From everyone to whom much has been given, much will be required; and from the one to whom much has been entrusted, even more will be demanded" (Luke 12:48).

Twenty-first-century Americans are among those fortunate ones who have been given much. People who live in a free country, with many opportunities for learning and serving, must heed this warning. We must glorify God by demonstrating his character and attitudes and actions in our own lives. We must teach all the lessons that Jesus taught by speaking his words and sharing his message. Finally, we must use every resource we have, including time, talents, skills, and money to spread the kingdom of God by making God's presence real throughout the world.

Jesus was a living, breathing representative of God. He came to give us a true picture of our Creator. He made us responsible for bringing in the kingdom. Knowing Jesus's life purposes will enable us to find and fill our own role in God's kingdom. It will also help us to know Jesus better and to become more like him.

Chapter 12

Jesus Defined the Duties of the Church

Jesus said, "I came to bear witness to the truth," one of which was to define the duties of the church.

Jesus said, "I will build my church, and the gates of Hades will not prevail against it" (Matt 16:18). Notice that Jesus said "my church." The church doesn't belong to a denomination or an organization. It doesn't belong to a domineering pastor. It doesn't belong to the elders or the deacons. It doesn't belong to a few big givers. It doesn't even belong to the voting majority. It's not Peter's church or Paul's church.

So there are some things a church must not do! A group of imperfect people must not establish creeds or resolutions or bylaws concerning the beliefs of the members. They must not set requirements or prohibitions about the actions and behavior of the members. They must not make rules and regulations about who can and who can't belong.

The church is not here to judge. The church is not here to condemn. The church is not here to punish. Since no one is without sin, then no one is qualified to punish. Instead of judging, condemning, or punishing, the church is to be a unifying force for righteousness. And in the church, everyone is equal: "There is no longer Jew or Greek, there is no longer slave or free, there is no longer male and female; for all of you are one in Christ Jesus" (Gal 3:28). It's obvious that Jesus wants all Christians to work together.

Since Jesus said, "This is my church," there are several things a church must do: First, it must seek the lost. That was Jesus's main purpose. This means we're to have a universal outreach. We're to invite, welcome, and receive all honest seekers. The parables of the lost sheep and the lost coin illustrate this fact. Jesus said, "Go therefore into the main streets, and invite everyone you find to the wedding banquet" (Matt 22:9). He issued a universal invitation to all nations and all races, saying, "People will come from east and west, from north and south, and will eat in the kingdom of God" (Luke 13:29). Remember, eating together indicated social equality and fellowship.

Next, the church must be sure to preach what Jesus preached and teach what Jesus taught. These teachings include his sermons, his lessons, and his conversations. People often gathered to hear him.

The leaders were disturbed with Jesus's teachings. Indeed, they were insistent and said, "He stirs up the people by teaching throughout all Judea, from Galilee where he began even to this place" (Luke 23:5). So the church must teach.

Above all, the church must maintain a harmonious and loving atmosphere. Members must treat each other as spiritual brothers and sisters. Jesus said, "Be at peace with one another" (Mark 9:50). Nothing harms the cause of Christ as much as conflict and disharmony within the church. In fact, love is the criteria by which the world will evaluate the church and its members.

It's also the duty of the church to counsel, encourage, and support its members. Jesus described all the services the church must provide when he said, "I was hungry and you gave me food, I was thirsty and you gave me something to drink, I was a stranger and you welcomed me, I was naked and you gave me clothing, I was sick and you took care of me, I was in prison and you visited me" (Matt 25:35–36). When we help those in need, we're serving Jesus.

The church fills a vital role in society. Jesus said, "You are the salt of the earth; but if salt has lost its taste, how can its saltiness be restored?

It is no longer good for anything, but is thrown out and trampled under foot" (Matt 5:13). Salt makes things better. Salt preserves things. Salt is essential for life.

Jesus also said, "You are the light of the world.... Let your light shine before others" (Matt 5:14, 16). Light offers knowledge and information. Light dispels darkness and ignorance. Light provides direction. The world has never needed this more than it does today! A polarized, fragmented, and alienated population is desperate for guidance and hope.

Successful churches enrich and improve their neighborhoods and communities. The church must not neglect its tasks. It must not shirk its duties. It must not forget its mandate. It must not be distracted by trivial matters. The church that Jesus established fills needs that no other organization can fill.

Jesus wants his church to be a hospital for sinners: "Those who are well have no need of a physician, but those who are sick" (Matt 9:12). He wants his church to be a haven for the weary: "Come to me, all you that are weary and are carrying heavy burdens, and I will give you rest" (Matt 11:28). He wants his church to be a sanctuary for the troubled: "Peace I leave with you; my peace I give to you.... Do not let your hearts be troubled, and do not let them be afraid" (John 14:27).

In short, the church is to say all the things that Jesus said and do all the things that Jesus did. It is here to proclaim his message and to carry out his ministry. It is here to give members an opportunity to fulfill leadership roles, to participate in benevolent projects, to enjoy social fellowship, and to have inspiring worship experiences. Yes, Jesus said, "I will build my church." And he left the church here to bless the world. God is present in each church in a special way. Jesus said, "Where two or three are gathered in my name, I am there among them" (Matt 18:20).

All believers have both a duty and a privilege to appreciate, support, and cherish this gift. Jesus promised that the church would have a great and productive future. He assured us through the parable of the mustard seed that no power can defeat it (see Mark 4:31–32).

Jesus loved the church. The scriptures give us an unforgettable picture of his relationship with the church, saying, "Christ loved the church and gave himself up for her…so as to present the church…without a spot or wrinkle or anything of the kind—yes, so that she may be holy and without blemish" (Eph 5:25, 27).

Jesus told us what the church must not do and what the church must do! If we heed his advice, this will help us carry out his ministry and achieve his purpose, which will help us to know him better and to become more like him.

At Jerusalem's Pool of Bethesda Jesus healed a paralyzed man, as recounted in the fifth chapter of the Gospel of John. The appearance of the pool changed over the centuries following the time of Jesus as additional construction covered up the pool as it existed in the New Testament era.
—*Photo copyright Bruce Gourley*

Conclusion

A Profile of Jesus

Few profiles of Jesus's personality have ever been attempted. But the Gospels do give us some glimpses of his childhood, his feelings, his thoughts, his words, and his deeds.

As a child he was intelligent and independent. When he was scolded after being lost for three days in Jerusalem, he pushed back. As an adult he began to reveal his feelings. We can discover what made him angry, what made him sad, what made him happy, what evoked his sympathy.

Jesus absolutely despised hypocrisy and did not hesitate to express his views. He definitely condemned greed, as evidenced in his dealings with Zacchaeus and the rich young ruler. He was also impatient with people's lack of concern.

Jesus also felt deep grief and had periods of depression. But he could also be joyful and often celebrated with his disciples.

Overall, Jesus was a caring, compassionate person with a loving heart. He was thoughtful and logical. He encouraged others to think for themselves.

Almost all of Jesus's words in his sermons, teachings, and conversations dealt with developing character, maintaining relationships, and deepening spirituality. He advised us to build our lives on a rock, with a stable and permanent foundation. He emphasized good social relationships. He even indicated that reconciliation with others takes precedence over worship. He advised us to avoid negative gossip and criticism of others, instead urging us to improve ourselves. He commanded tolerance and absolute forgiveness.

All of Jesus's deeds dealt with healing, helping, and comforting people who were hurting and confused. Many stereotypes of Jesus leave the impression that he was a pious idealist, but he was actually a practical man who used common sense. He was not an "otherworldly" religious fanatic like many of the prophets. Ordinary people liked him; children came to him; sinners discovered that he was their friend.

When Jesus was questioned by Pilate, he stated the purpose of his mission, saying, "For this I was born, and for this I came into the world, to testify to the truth" (John 18:37). Jesus came to clear up misconceptions about the nature of God, explaining that our creator is not a physical entity. He also said God is loving and forgiving, not threatening and vengeful. He understood that God is within us, not somewhere "out there" in space.

Jesus gave us advice about how to handle evil. He instructed us not to judge and condemn. He also disapproved of attacks and criticism. He explained that these methods do more harm than good. Instead of fighting evil, we must replace it with good and live the law of love. Jesus did not establish a religion of rules and regulations.

Jesus reinterpreted the power of redemption. He described it as a wonderful gift that fills our need for acceptance, value, security, forgiveness, and purpose. We are accepted. We are valued. We are secure. We are forgiven. We have a purpose.

Jesus taught that concern for others is the basis of the Christian life. He illustrated concern in most of his parables and gave dire warnings to those who neglect hurting people. He elevated men and women to a new level.

Jesus demanded responsibility, insisting that we are God's agents for change. We are absolutely accountable for the success or failure of life on this earth. As Christians we must abolish the darkness of ignorance, negligence, and hostility.

Jesus clearly defined the mission of his church, enumerating the dos and don'ts of this important institution. The church is here to teach, to inspire, to provide opportunities for fellowship, benevolence, and worship. It is to be a hospital for sinners and a sanctuary for the wounded and oppressed. The church is definitely not here to judge, condemn, or punish. Jesus said only perfect people are capable of doing that, and no one is perfect.

Jesus promised his protection for the church. Even more importantly, he promised his presence in the church. Jesus said, "Remember, I am with you always, to the end of the age" (Matt 28:20).